cloverleaf books™

Fall's Here!

W9-BCO-478

Fall Apples

Crisp and Juicy

Martha E. H. Rustad

illustrated by Amanda Enright

M MILLBROOK PRESS · MINNEAPOLIS

For my parents — M.E.H.R.
For Lily and Oliver — A.E.

Millbrook Press
A division of Lerner Publishing Group, Inc.
241 First Avenue North
Minneapolis, MN 55401 U.S.A.

Website address: www.lernerbooks.com

Main body text set in Slappy Inline 18/28.
Typeface provided by T26.

Library of Congress Cataloging-in-Publication Data

Rustad, Martha E. H. (Martha Elizabeth Hillman), 1975–
    Fall apples : crisp and juicy / by Martha E. H. Rustad ;
  illustrated by Amanda Enright.
        p.   cm.
    Includes index.
    ISBN: 978–0–7613–5064–4 (lib. bdg. : alk. paper)
    1. Apples—Juvenile literature. 2. Apples—Harvesting—
Juvenile literature. 3. Cooking (Apples)—Juvenile literature.
I. Enright, Amanda, ill. II. Title.
SB363.R37 2012
634'.11—dc22   2010051510

Manufactured in the United States of America
1 – BP – 7/15/11

JUVENILE

Schaumburg Township District Library
130 South Roselle Road
Schaumburg, Illinois 60193

CENTRAL

TABLE OF CONTENTS

Chapter One

Apples in Fall

Look! Colorful leaves blow in the breeze. The air feels cooler. **It is fall.**

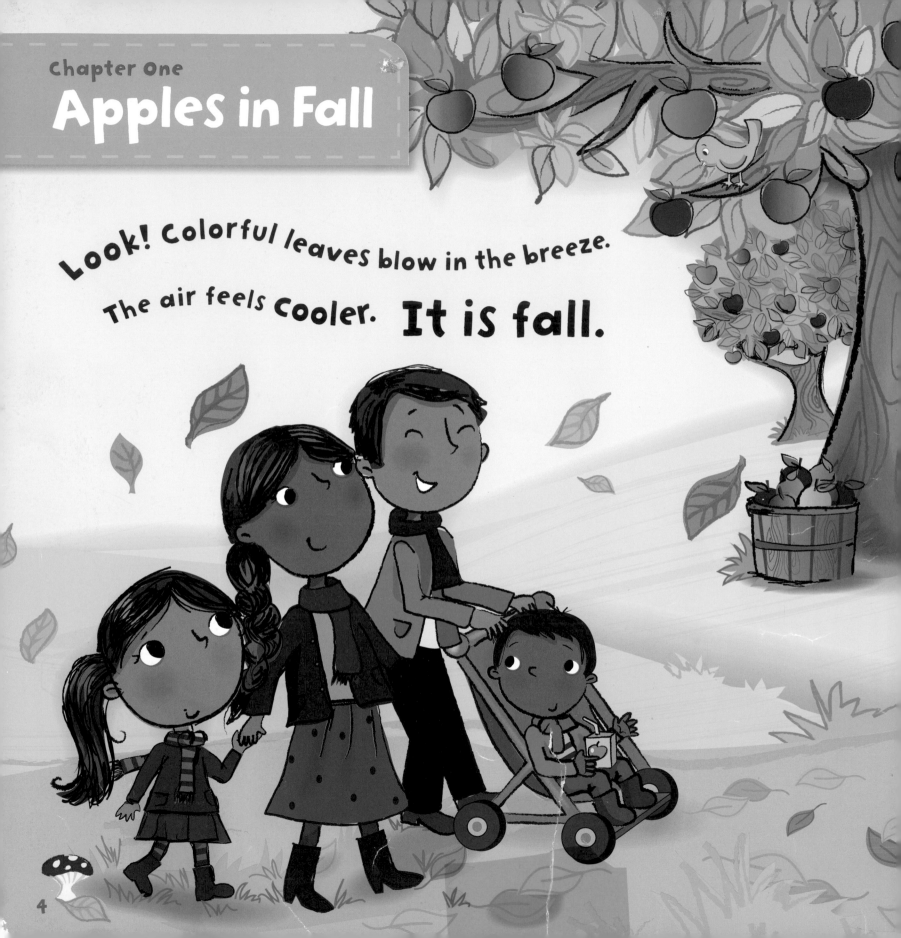

Fall is a good time to visit an **apple orchard.** Fall is a good time to pick apples.

Welcome to
Apple Tree
ORCHARD

Orchards around the world grow about fifty kinds of apples.

Crunch!

I bite through the red skin. The crisp, white flesh tastes sweet. Juice drips down my chin.

Surprise! Tiny dark seeds hide inside the core.

Most ripe apples have red skin. Some have yellow or green skin.

Chapter Two

How Apples Grow

Plop! An apple seed falls into the soil. Roots grow down. A stem grows up.

Drip! Just enough **rain** helps the seed become a sprout.

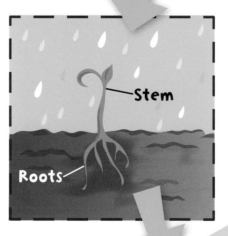

Stem

Roots

Just enough **sunlight** helps the sprout become a tree.

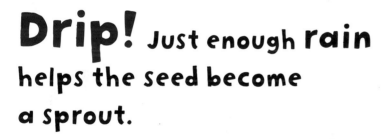

When an apple seed grows into a tree, its apples are different from the apple that made the seed. To grow a certain kind of apple, orchards attach a stem from one tree to the roots of another. Then they grow together.

Green leaves **bud** and **spread.**
Leaves soak up warm sunlight.

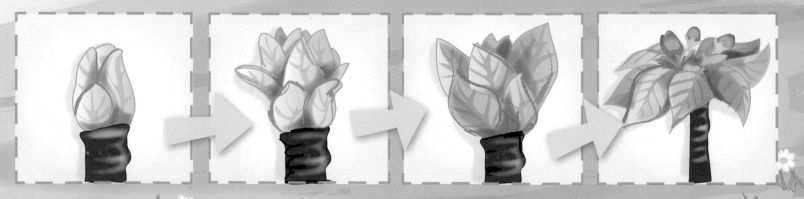

Sunlight becomes **food** for the growing tree.

Some trees start to grow apples three to five years after they are planted.

Sniff!

I smell the sweet flowers. In the spring, white and pink **apple blossoms** bloom.

BUZZ! Bees drink **nectar** from apple flowers. **Pollen** from the flowers sticks to their bodies. Bees spread pollen from tree to tree.

Apple blossoms need pollen from another kind of apple tree to grow fruit. Bees and other insects spread pollen from the flowers on one tree to the flowers on another tree.

Pollen from another tree fertilizes the flowers. Then their **petals** fall.

Tiny green **fruitlets** form.

During the summer, fruitlets grow into **big apples.**

Pickers harvest apples in fall. Ripe apples pile up.

Apple pickers are gentle. They twist off only the apple and stem. No apple will grow there the next year if they pull off the spur that connects the stem to the tree.

Chapter Three

Using Apples

Let's visit the orchard's kitchen. Bakers peel, core, and cut apples to make pies.

Ding!
The pie is done.

It smells like **cinnamon** and **baked apples**.
My teeth crush the **crisp crust**.

About half of the U.S. apple crop is eaten fresh. People make the rest into jelly, cider, juice, vinegar, apple butter, applesauce, or pie filling.

Jelly

Let's make apple cider.

About forty apples are pressed to make 1 gallon (3.8 liters) of apple cider.

Apple Cider

Apple Cider

Whir! The grinder turns. It smashes the apples into pulp.

Apple
Cider

Squish! The press squeezes the apple pulp. Cider trickles out.

We drink the cider.
It looks cloudier
than apple juice.

It tastes **sweet** and **tart.** Yum!

Apple juice makers
heat and filter cider
to make juice.

Good-bye, orchard!
Let's visit again next fall.

Welcome to
Apple Tree
ORCHARD

Upside-Down, Inside-Out Apple Crisp Recipe

Ask an adult for help in the kitchen.

Ingredients:
1 small apple
1 teaspoon quick-cooking oatmeal
1/8 teaspoon salt
1 teaspoon brown sugar
1/8 teaspoon cinnamon
1/2 teaspoon butter
1/2 teaspoon maple syrup

Equipment:
melon baller
microwave-safe bowl
measuring spoons
cover for bowl or plastic wrap
microwave
oven mitts

1) Wash your apple well. Remove the stem. Turn the apple upside down. Use the melon baller to core the apple. Stop just before going all the way through the end of the apple.

2) Place the apple in the microwave-safe bowl. Put the oatmeal, salt, brown sugar, cinnamon, butter, and syrup inside the apple core. Try not to overfill the apple.

3) Cover the bowl with the lid or plastic wrap. Cook it in the microwave for 2 minutes. Remove the bowl with the oven mitts. Let the bowl sit with the cover on for 2 more minutes.

4) Remove the cover. Eat your upside-down, inside-out apple crisp!

GLOSSARY

blossom: a tiny flower on a tree

bud: to form a bud. A bud is a part of a plant or tree that grows into a leaf or a flower.

fertilize: to make a new fruit grow by putting pollen into a flower

filter: to put a liquid through a strainer and remove anything floating in the liquid

flesh: the part of a fruit you can eat. The flesh of ripe apples is most often white. It can also be yellow, pink, or green.

fruitlet: a young or tiny fruit. Fruitlets grow and ripen into fruit.

harvest: to gather crops that are ripe. Orchards harvest ripe apples in fall.

nectar: a sweet liquid found in flowers. Bees drink and gather nectar to make honey.

orchard: a farm that grows fruit trees

pollen: a tiny yellow dust made by flowers. Apple flowers need pollen from another flower to make seeds.

roots: parts of a plant or tree that grow underground

soil: dirt or earth. Plants grow in soil.

sprout: a new plant that has just started to grow

spur: a tiny part that grows out of a tree branch

stem: the long main part of a plant. Leaves and flowers grow from the stem.

trunk: the woody stem of a tree

TO LEARN MORE

BOOKS

Nelson, Robin. *Apple Trees.* Minneapolis: Lerner Publications Company, 2009.
Simple text and photographs show the life cycle of an apple tree.

Purmell, Ann. *Apple Cider Making Days.* Minneapolis: Millbrook Press, 2002.
This picture book tells the story of a family who harvests apples on their orchard
and makes apple cider.

Smucker, Anna Egan. *Golden Delicious: A Cinderella Apple Story.* Morton Grove, IL:
Albert Whitman, 2008. Read about how the Golden Delicious apple was first discovered more
than one hundred years ago in West Virginia.

Snyder, Inez. *Apples.* New York: Children's Press, 2004.
Text and photographs show how apples are grown and harvested.

WEBSITES

American Fruit Processors: Apple Juice Fun and Games
http://www.applejuice.org/fungames.html
You can visit this site to read about Johnny Appleseed, play games, and find crossword puzzles.

U.S. Apple Association: Apple Wise Guys Coloring Book
http://www.usapple.org/consumers/kids/coloring.cfm
This site has a coloring book you can download that teaches about different kinds of apples.

Washington Apple Commission: Crispy's Apple Stand
http://www.bestapples.com/kids/home.shtml
On this site, you can learn about apples, play a trivia game, and find apple recipes.

INDEX